PROPHET OF PEACE
Prophet Muhammad for Little Hearts

by
Nafees Khan

Goodword**kidz**
Helping you build a family of faith

2

I'll tell you a story
Of a Prophet of Peace ﷺ
Who lost his dear mother
When he was a little child

3

4

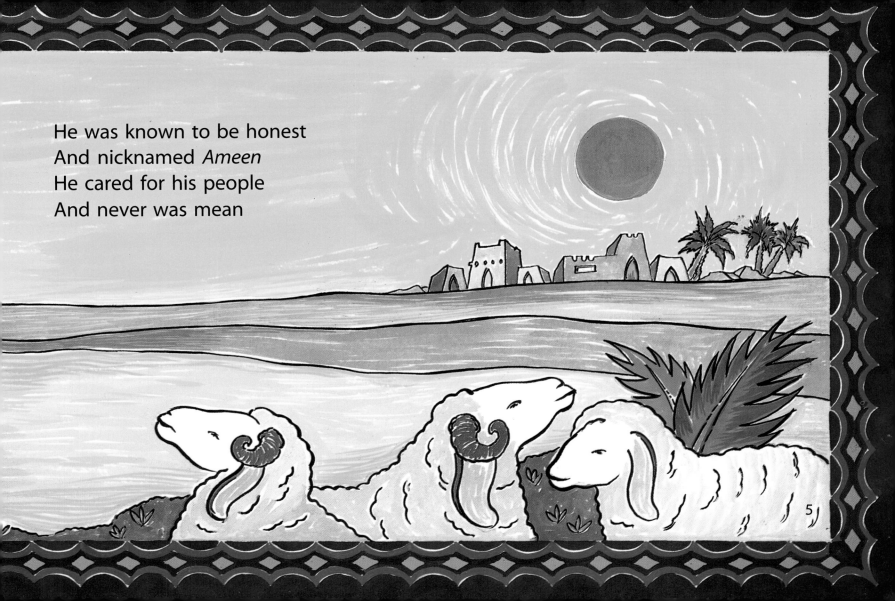

He was known to be honest
And nicknamed *Ameen*
He cared for his people
And never was mean

5

He prayed in the mountains
Alone in the cave
And until one Ramadan
When the angel Jibril came

He ran to Khadijah
And straight to his bed
His body was shaking
There was sweat on his head

8

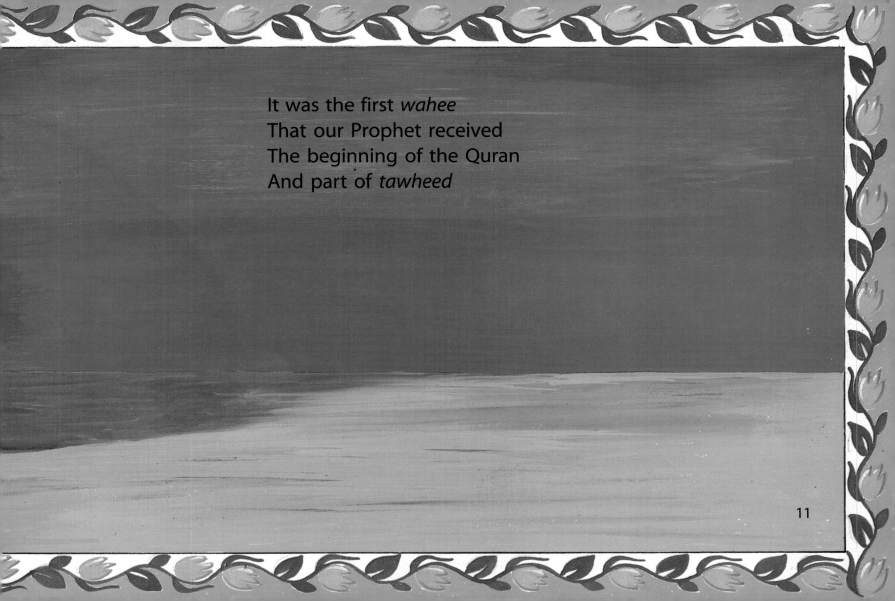

It was the first *wahee*
That our Prophet received
The beginning of the Quran
And part of *tawheed*

When he started his message
The Makkans didn't believe
They tortured his people
And forced them to leave

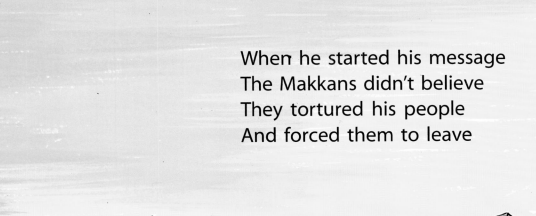

He went to Madinah
Along with Siddiq
The Ansars of Yathrib
Were so very pleased

15

He received Allah's message
Till he was sixty and three
There are 114 *surahs*
In Quran al Hakeem

18

He taught us the *Kalimah*
That says there's one God
Muhammad ﷺ is the messenger
And slave of our Lord

If you love Allah
Don't ever do *Kufr*
Hold on to your *iman*
And always be good

21

So practice his *Sunnah*
And read the Quran
I told you the story
Of the Prophet of Peace ﷺ

23

Even if you are ninety
You still will be mine
So pray for my *maghfirah*
And for Him to be kind.

24